Cuisines from

Arushi Mahajan

A Sterling Paperback

STERLING PAPERBACKS
An imprint of
Sterling Publishers (P) Ltd.
A-59, Okhla Industrial Area, Phase-II, New Delhi-110020
Ph. : 6387070, 6386209, Fax : 91-11-6383788
E-mail: ghai@nde.vsnl.net.in

Cuisines from the World
©2003, Sterling Publishers (P) Ltd.
ISBN 81 207 2486 0

All rights are reserved. No part of this publication may be reproduced, stored in a retrieval system or transmitted, in any form or by any means, mechanical, photocopying, recording or otherwise, without prior written permission of the publisher.

Published by Sterling Publishers Pvt. Ltd., New Delhi-110020.
Lasertypeset by Vikas Compographics, New Delhi-110020.
Printed at Baba Barkha Nath Printers, New Delhi.

About the book

Unique in its breadth and perspective, this book brings out the taste and flavour of six cuisines from all over the world – Chinese, Continental, Indian, Italian, Mexican and Thai. Each cuisine contains vegetarian recipes representing varied menu options. One can choose from starters, soups, main courses and delectable desserts.

Cooking is an art and patience a virtue... Careful shopping, fresh ingredients and an unhurried approach are nearly all you need. There is one more thing — love: love for food and for those you invite to your table. The recipes have been crafted in such a way that they are practical, easy to follow and interesting, and will provide you with the opportunity to cook delicious, mouth-watering vegetarian meals. The main emphasis of the book is on vegetarian food. Vegetarian food provides all essential nutrients and is ample in proteins.

Most of the ingredients used are easily available, and explained in the glossary.

The weights and measures used are standard.

Dry measures: 1 cup = 200 gms, 1 tsp = 5 gms, 1 tbsp = 15 gms

Liquid measures: 1 cup = 200 ml

Attractively designed and illustrated with colour photographs, this book will prove to be a valuable aid in developing your culinary knowledge and expertise.

Good luck and happy cooking!

To my parents
and the other members of my family,
for their constant encouragement and support,
and for their untiring efforts in helping me
create this book

Contents

Glossary	6
Chinese	9
Continental	27
Indian	47
Italian	66
Mexican	86
Thai	108

Glossary

Ajinomoto - Monosodium glutamate, commonly known as Chinese salt
Almond - Badam
Aniseed - Saunf
Aubergine, Eggplant - Brinjal
Basil - Tulsi
Bay leaf - Tej patta
Bean sprouts - There are two kinds of bean sprouts - one is made out of soya bean and the other out of green gram (whole moong)
Brown sugar - Shakkar
Burfi - An Indian sweet made from thickened milk and sugar
Cardamom - Elaichi
Cashewnut - Kaju
Castor sugar - Powdered sugar
Cinnamon - Dalchini
Clove - Laung
Coriander - Dhaniya
Cottage cheese - Paneer
Cumin - Zeera
Dried mango powder - Amchoor
Flour - Maida
Galangal - A kind of Thai ginger
Garam masala - Powdered whole spices
Ghee - Clarified butter
Gram - Chane
Gramflour - Besan
Kasoori methi - Dried fenugreek leaves
Keema - Mince
Khus - Poppy seeds
Lemon grass - An aromatic lemon-flavoured herb used mainly in Thai curry pastes

Lentil - Masoor dal
Lettuce - Cabbage
Lotus root - Kamal kakri
Melon seeds - Magaz
Mint - Pudina
Mustard - Rai / Sarson
Nachos - A Mexican dish of crisp pieces of tortillas
Nutmeg - Jaiphal
Okra - Bhindi
Oregano - An aromatic herb
Parsley - Ajmoda ka patta
Peanut - Moongphali
Pepper - Kali mirch
Rajma - Kidney beans
Saffron - Kesar
Semolina - Suji
Sesame seeds - Til
Soda-bi-carb - Meetha soda
Spinach - Palak
Spring onions - Hara Pyaz
Thyme - Hasha
Turmeric - Haldi
Vark - Edible silver foil
Walnut - Akhrot
Wheat flour - Atta

Boiled noodles: Take the required amount of noodles, for e.g. 1 packet chow noodles, add 5 cups of boiling water, with ½ tsp oil and a dash of salt. Cook for 5 minutes and drain under cold water. Add 1 tsp oil to the noodles to avoid sticking.

Curry powder or Kitchen King masala: A blend of salt, zeera powder, cinnamon, nutmeg powder, cardamom, peppercorns and artificial flavourings.

Fish sauce: It is a Thai sauce of two kinds – vegetarian and non-vegetarian. Vegetable fish sauce has been used in this book, and is easily available in the market.

Glass noodles: String-like fine, dried, transparent noodles.

Green curry paste: 1 tbsp coriander seeds, 2 tsp cumin seeds, 1 tsp black peppercorn, 2 tsp vegetable fish sauce, 1 cup chopped onion, 2 tbsp oil, 2 tsp salt, 6 lime leaves or basil leaves, 5" piece galangal, 1 cup fresh coriander leaves, 2 tbsp garlic paste, 1 tsp green food colour, 8 large green chillies. Blend all the ingredients into a paste.

Hung curd: Take required quantity of curd in a muslin cloth. Hang to let the water drain (for about 20 minutes).

Red curry paste: 1 tbsp coriander seeds, 2 tsp cumin seeds, 1 tsp black peppercorn, 1 tsp ground nutmeg, 1 cup chopped onion, 2 tsp turmeric, 1 tsp chilli powder, 2 tsp salt, 2 tsp grated lemon rind, 2 tbsp fresh coriander, 2 tsp garlic paste, 2 tbsp oil, 4 stems lemon grass, 1 tsp vegetable fish sauce. Blend all the ingredients into a paste.

Vegetable stock: Makes 5 cups – 1 cup mixed, sliced vegetables, 6 cups of water, 1 tsp ginger paste, ½ tsp salt, 1 onion, finely chopped. Mix all the ingredients and pressure cook for 5 minutes after the first whistle. Cool and strain.

White sauce: Makes 2 cups – 2 tbsp flour, 2 tbsp butter, 2½ cups milk, salt and pepper to taste. Heat the butter in a pan, add the flour and saute for 2 minutes. Gradually add the milk, stirring continuously to avoid lumps. Season with salt and pepper.

CHINESE

"Cookery is not chemistry. It is an art, it requires instinct and taste rather than exact measurements."
– Marcel Boulestin

China is a country where the preparation and appreciation of food has been developed to the highest level. For the Chinese, food and friends are inseparable. A gathering without food is considered incomplete and improper. Chinese lay stress on the use of colour and texture in the presentation of the dish. They believe that good cooking depends on the blending of various ingredients rather than the taste of the individual elements. Unlike the majority of eastern cuisines, most Chinese dishes are low in calories and fat. Milk, cream, butter and cheese are not part of their daily diet, hence Chinese cooking is healthy cooking.

Menu

- Dragon Roll   (Starter)
- Manchow Soup   (Soup)
- Kimchi Salad   (Salad)
- Braised Aubergines   (Main course)
- Crispy Chilli Honey Lotus Root   (Main course)
- Banana Toffee   (Dessert)

← *Dragon Roll (p 12)*

Chinese

Dragon Roll

Serves 8

Ingredients

8 pieces of bread, with edges trimmed
3 tsp very finely chopped ginger, garlic and coriander
1 cup mixed vegetables (carrot, French beans, cabbage, capsicum), very finely chopped
1 tbsp soya sauce
1 tsp ajinomoto
1 tsp chilli paste or chilli sauce
½ cup onions, chopped
Oil for deep frying
2 tsp cornflour mixed with 4 tbsp water, to make a paste
4 tsp roasted sesame seeds
Salt and pepper to taste

How to make the flour mixture

1. Mix 4 tablespoons of flour with ½ cup water or as required, to have a thick consistency.
2. The water should be added to the flour slowly to avoid the mixture from becoming too watery.

Method

1. Heat a pan and pour in 1 tablespoon oil. Then add the chopped ginger, garlic, coriander and onions and cook for 5 minutes.
2. Add salt and pepper and all the sauces and then all the vegetables. Cook for 2 minutes. Cool the mixture. Keep aside.
3. Now take a vessel with 2 glasses of water and put it on the flame. When the water starts boiling keep a strainer on top of the vessel.
4. Now take each bread slice and steam it on the vessel.

Chinese

5. Immediately roll each steamed bread slice with a rolling pin, so that it becomes softer and thinner.
6. Place the vegetable filling on one side of the slice and make it into rolls.
7. Seal the edges with the cornflour paste. Cut them as desired. Dip it in the flour mixture and then deep fry.
8. Serve on a flat plate, garnished with lotus roots, capsicums, etc.

Manchow Soup

Serves 6

Ingredients

½ cup very finely chopped cabbage
½ cup very finely chopped carrot
½ cup very finely chopped mushrooms
½ cup very finely chopped French beans
¼ cup chopped tomatoes
1 tbsp each of chopped ginger, green chillies and coriander.
2 tsp ajinomoto
1 tbsp soya sauce
Cornflour paste (1 tbsp cornflour mixed with 2 tbsp water)
Salt and pepper to taste

Method

1. Take 6 cups water, add all the vegetables (except the tomatoes and cabbage) and boil till soft.
2. Drain the vegetables and reserve the stock.
3. Take 1 tablespoon oil and saute the ginger, chilli, coriander and tomatoes for 5 minutes.
4. Now add all the vegetables and saute for 5 more minutes. Then add 1 cup stock, and the soya sauce, ajinomoto and salt and pepper.
5. Bring to the boil and add the rest of the stock and the cornflour paste. Stir well to mix the cornflour paste.
6. Bring to the boil on medium heat.
7. Garnish this soup with the noodles at the time of serving.

How to make fried noodles

Take half a packet of chow noodles. Boil and then let it drain for half an hour. Now sprinkle a handful of flour so that the noodles are well coated. Fry these noodles in very hot oil till crisp.

Chinese

Kimchi Salad

Serves 6

Ingredients

1 pkt chow noodles, boiled and deep fried
½ cup cabbage, thinly sliced (lengthwise)
½ cup onions, cut lengthwise
½ cup capsicum, cut lengthwise

For the dressing

4 tbsp salad oil
2 tbsp vinegar
A pinch of red colour
½ tsp freshly ground green chilli paste
A pinch of mustard powder
Salt and pepper to taste

Method

1. Mix all the ingredients for the dressing and shake well. Keep aside.
2. Add the dressing to the vegetables and noodles and serve immediately.

Note:
- *The taste of the salad is spicy. Spices can be adjusted according to taste.*
- *The noodles should be fried in the same way as given on page 18.*
- *The crispy noodles should be added only at the time of serving.*

Chinese

Braised Aubergines

Serves 6

Ingredients

2 large aubergines, cut into 2" strips
Oil for shallow frying
1 tsp garlic, sliced
2 tbsp dried sherry or port wine
4 spring onions, sliced
2 tsp ginger, shredded
2 tbsp soya sauce
2 tbsp chilli sauce
1 tbsp roasted sesame seeds
Chopped red and green chillies for garnishing

← *Banana Toffee (p 25)*

Method

1. Heat 2 tablespoons of oil in a wok or deep frying pan.
2. Add the spring onions, garlic and ginger and stir fry for about 30 seconds.
3. Remove from the pan and keep aside.
4. Increase the heat, add the aubergine strips and fry until brown, adding more oil to the pan if necessary.
5. Remove from the pan and drain the strips on the kitchen paper.
6. Pour off the oil from the pan into some other container.
7. Return the spring onions, garlic, ginger and aubergine strips to the pan.
8. Pour the soya sauce, sherry and chilli sauce on this, stir well and cook for 2 minutes.
9. Spoon into a warmed serving dish. Garnish with the chillies and sesame seeds and serve immediately.

Note:
- *Add salt to the cut aubergine strips. Drain for an hour. Discard the water.*

Crispy Chilli Honey Lotus Root

Serves 8

Ingredients

2 lotus roots, properly washed and thinly sliced
2 onions, diced
2 capsicums, diced
5 pieces red whole chilli (dry), deseeded
½ cup finely chopped onions
1 tbsp finely chopped ginger
2 tbsp garlic, 1 tbsp chilli sauce
1½ tbsp tomato sauce
1 tsp honey
1½ tsp ajinomoto
A pinch of red colour, salt to taste

Method

1. Take the lotus roots, coat with a handful of cornflour and a handful of flour, sprinkle a little water and then deep fry till crisp. Keep aside.
2. Now pour the oil into a pan, add the broken dry chilli pieces, finely chopped onions, ginger and garlic and saute for 5 minutes.
3. Add the capsicum and broadly diced onions, cook on high flame till crisp. Then add all the sauces, ajinomoto, colour and salt. Toss over high flame for 2 minutes. Add the fried lotus. Add the honey. Mix well.
4. Serve hot immediately.

Note:
- *Mix the fried lotus roots only at the time of serving or else it gets soggy.*

Banana Toffee

Serves 6

Ingredients

4 ripe bananas
½ cup flour
1 tsp cinnamon powder
½ tsp baking powder
2 tsp oil
1 tbsp powder sugar
Juice of 1 lemon (large)
2 tsp honey (optional)
½ cup milk (approx.)

Method

1. Peel and cut the bananas into 2 pieces longitudinally, or in rounds and then crosswise to get 4 pieces from each banana.
2. Sprinkle the cinnamon, lemon juice and 1 tablespoon sugar on them.
3. Make a batter with the flour, oil, milk, honey and baking powder. The batter should not be very thin in consistency.
4. Mix well till smooth.
5. Heat the oil. Dip the banana slices in the batter and fry till golden brown.
6. Heat some sugar in a pan till it caramelises, making sure it does not get burnt. Coat the fried bananas with this sugar syrup.
7. Then place the banana pieces on a bowlful of ice till the sugar crystallises. Remove them from the ice bowl and keep aside.
8. Serve warm with vanilla ice-cream.

CONTINENTAL

"Good cookery is the food of a pure conscience."
– Des Essarts

There is a tendency to confuse Continental cooking with elaborate cooking. Yet nothing could be further from the truth. There are elaborate dishes as well as simple dishes. Basic dishes gain a subtlety of flavour from the addition of wine, herbs, cheese, mushrooms and vinegar. The ingredients are rich in texture and taste. White sauce is the basic sauce used, and butter and milk play a vital role. In these pages you will find both sophisticated haute cuisine and simple fare.

Menu

- Cream of Mushroom   (Soup)
- Rice Salad   (Salad)
- Corn and Mushroom Pancakes   (Main course)
- Veg Florentine   (Main course)
- Baby Corn in Lemon Butter Sauce   (Main course)
- Mango Marvel   (Dessert)

Rice Salad (p 33) →

Cream of Mushroom Soup

Serves 6

Ingredients

250 gms mushrooms, coarsely chopped
2 tbsp vinegar
5 cups of water
1 cup white sauce
2 tbsp garlic juice
Salt and pepper to taste

For garnishing

6 tbsp cream
1 tbsp finely chopped coriander
100 gms mushrooms, cut lengthwise

← *Cream of Mushroom*

Method

1. Chop and wash the mushrooms. Pour the water and vinegar into a pan and add the mushrooms to it. Boil for 3 minutes and simmer till the mushrooms become soft.
2. Add the garlic juice and salt and pepper and keep on heat. Cook for 5 minutes.
3. Add one cup white sauce and mix well. Stir continuously so that the white sauce does not curdle. Cook well. Boil for 5-10 minutes.
4. Add the mushrooms, coriander and cream.

Rice Salad

Serves 6

Ingredients

---

1 ½ cups cooked plain boiled rice
*(The rice should be boiled in such a way that
the grains should be separate and not sticky)*
½ cup chopped onions
½ cup diced yellow bell capsicum
4 tbsp coarsely chopped carrots
4 tbsp finely chopped cabbage
½ cup peanuts

For the dressing

1 tbsp vinegar
½ tsp French mustard/powder mustard
2 pinches of salt
A pinch of sugar
A pinch of pepper
1 garlic clove, crushed
4 tbsp salad oil

Mix all the ingredients, blend well and refrigerate.

Method

1. Mix all the ingredients with the dressing and serve chilled on a bed of lettuce leaves.

Corn and Mushroom Pancakes

Makes 6-8

Ingredients

For the pancakes

150 gms flour
250 ml liquid (water and milk, in the ratio of 1:1)
1 tbsp melted butter
A pinch of salt
¼ tsp soda-bi-carb

For the white sauce

3 cups milk
2 tbsp butter, 2 tbsp flour
¾ tsp salt, ½ tsp pepper

For the stuffing

2 tbsp butter
1 ½ onions, finely chopped
500 gms mushrooms, chopped
1 tbsp garlic paste
1 cup corn kernels
5 tbsp grated cheese
2 tbsp cream
Salt and red chilli powder to taste
A few tomato rings for garnishing

Method

1. To prepare the batter for the pancakes, sift the flour and salt together.
2. Then add enough of the liquid, containing milk and water, to get a thin pouring consistency. Add the butter. Mix well. Make sure no lumps are formed.

3. Heat a non-stick pan. Smear 1 teaspoon oil in the centre. Remove the pan from the fire and pour a ladleful of the batter.
4. Tilt the pan to spread the batter. Return to the fire and cook till the underside gets done. Remove the pancake from the pan. Similarly make all the pancakes and keep aside.
5. To prepare the white sauce, melt the butter and add the flour. Stir for a minute on low flame. Add the milk, stirring continuously. Then add the salt and pepper. Cook till it starts to coat the spoon. Take it off the fire.
6. For the stuffing, heat the butter in a large pan. Add the onion, garlic and saute for a minute. Then add the chopped mushrooms, ½ teaspoon salt and ¼ teaspoon pepper, and cook for 3-4 minutes, till all the juices drawn from the mushrooms evaporate.
7. Add the corn and cook for 5 minutes. Then add the grated cheese and cream. Mix well. Add salt and red chilli powder to taste.

8. Divide the filling, according to the number of pancakes prepared. Take a pancake, spread one part of the filling in the centre. Cover the filling by folding the pancake once.

9. Take a big rectangular ovenproof dish. Spread ½ of the white sauce. Arrange the pancakes, slightly overlapping each other and with the joint side down.

10. Pour the remaining white sauce in the centre of the pancakes. Sprinkle the grated cheese. Garnish with the tomato rings.

11. Bake in a preheated oven at 180°C for 20 minutes and serve.

Veg Florentine

Serves 8

Ingredients

1 cup boiled and pureed spinach
500 gms of cottage cheese, cut into thick slabs
2 cups of white sauce
¾ cup tomatoes, finely chopped
¾ cup onions, finely chopped
1 tbsp garlic paste
2 tsp dried parsley, a pinch of nutmeg
1 tsp red chilli flakes
4 tbsp thick cream, 4 tbsp butter
100 gms of processed cheese
Salt and white pepper to taste

Method

1. Heat 2 tablespoons of the butter in a pan, add the spinach puree and cook on a low flame for 5 minutes.
2. Season with salt and pepper and the nutmeg. Keep aside.
3. Saute the garlic and onions in the remaining butter for 5 minutes.
4. Season with parsley.
5. Then add the tomatoes and cook further for 7-8 minutes on low flame.
6. Take it off the fire and keep the mix separately.
7. To arrange the dish, spread ½ of the white sauce at the base of an ovenproof dish. Then arrange ½ the cottage cheese slabs, top it up with the spinach mixture and then with the tomato mix.

← Veg Florentine (p 39)

8. Repeat this process of layering again in the same order, till all the mixture is consumed, with the cheese remaining as the top-most layer.
9. Bake at 200°C for ½ an hour, till well set.
10. Serve hot with fresh salad or a piece of bread.

Baby Corn in Lemon Butter Sauce

Serves 6

Ingredients

1 can baby corns (washed and drained)
2 onions, cut lengthwise
Juice of 2 lemons
6 tbsp of butter
A handful of chopped coriander
1 tsp red chilli flakes
1 tsp dried parsley
½ cup fresh cream
1 tbsp garlic paste
Salt and white pepper to taste

Method

1. Heat the butter in a pan, add the garlic paste and cook till it leaves a raw smell. Then add the onions and saute till transparent.
2. Add the baby corns and saute for 7-8 minutes.
3. Season the above mix with the chilli flakes, parsley and salt and pepper.
4. Add in the cream and bring to the boil.
5. Finally add in the lemon juice, cook for 2 minutes. Take it off the fire.
6. Serve hot.

Mango Marvel

Serves 8

Ingredients

12 bread slices (with edges trimmed), soaked in milk
2 mangoes, roughly chopped
Assorted nuts for garnishing
3 tbsp castor sugar
300 ml fresh cream
3 mangoes, chopped (for the filling)
½ cup chilled milk

Method

1. Blend the chopped mangoes, milk and sugar into a paste. Mix in the cream.
2. Now spread 2 tablespoons of this paste in a rectangular dish and layer it with 6 milk soaked bread slices.
3. On these bread slices arrange ½ the chopped mangoes kept aside for the filling. Then spread another layer of the mango paste, followed by the bread slices and the remaining chopped mangoes. Lastly, spread a thin layer of the mango paste.
4. Sprinkle the assorted nuts and serve chilled.

INDIAN

"The best way to win a man's heart is through his stomach."

Indian food is not limited to one style of cooking, rather it is an amalgamation of several cuisines representing different cultures and religious beliefs. Indian cooking is known for its use of spices, herbs and flavourings. The dishes range from mild to hot creamy curries. Many Indian dishes owe their fiery flavour to chillies, ginger and garlic. The subtle blend of herbs and spices gives each dish a unique flavour.

Indian

Menu

- Suji Dilkush   (Starter)
- Dal Shorba   (Soup)
- Mushroom-do-Pyaza   (Main course)
- Subz Biryani   (Main course)
- Aaloo Bahaar   (Main course)
- Khus Mehak   (Mocktail)
- Firnee   (Dessert)

Dal Shorba (p 52) →

Suji Dilkush

Serves 6

Ingredients

1 cup semolina
100 ml milk, 150 ml water
1½ tsp cumin seeds
2 onions, finely chopped
1 tsp fresh coriander, finely chopped
½ cup breadcrumbs
2 tbsp cornflour paste (2 tbsp cornflour mixed with 10 tbsp water to get a thin consistency paste)
½ tsp red chilli powder
3 tbsp refined oil
2 green chillies, finely chopped
Salt to taste

Method

1. Heat the oil in a pan, add the cumin, onions and green chillies and let it cook for 5 minutes. Take off the fire and keep aside.
2. Meanwhile, put the milk in a saucepan and bring to the boil. Add the water. Turn the flame to simmer and add the mix mentioned in step 1. Then add the salt, chilli powder and coriander and bring to the boil. Add the semolina and cook over medium flame, till it forms a ball or a thick lump.
3. Take it off the fire and let it cool for ½ an hour.
4. After it cools, take a flat bottomed plate, preferably a steel plate. Grease it well and spread this mixture on the plate. Keep it in the refrigerator for about 40 minutes.
5. Take it out from the refrigerator and cut the prepared set mixture diagonally to get squares. Take off the pieces carefully out of the plate.
6. Deep fry in very hot oil till crisp and golden brown.

Indian

Dal Shorba

Serves 6

Ingredients

1 cup lentil
2 medium onions, roughly chopped
1 potato, coarsely chopped
1 bay leaf
1 carrot, coarsely chopped
½ cup coriander leaves
1 tsp chopped garlic, 1 tsp ginger paste
¾ cup tomato puree
4 cups water
1 tbsp white vinegar
Salt to taste
Mint leaves and cream for garnishing

Method

1. Put all the ingredients in a cooker, except the vinegar, and stir.
2. Close the cooker, bring to full pressure on high flame. Reduce the flame and simmer for 15 minutes.
3. Remove the cooker from the heat and allow to cool naturally.
4. Open the cooker and discard the bay leaf. Put half the soup lightly in a blender.
5. Return the blended soup to the remaining soup in the cooker and add the vinegar. Stir and reheat. Serve hot garnished with the mint and a swirl of cream.

Note:
- *Make sure to add the vinegar only in the end.*

Indian

Mushroom-Do-Pyaza

Serves 6

Ingredients

1 pkt mushroom, boiled and cut into 4 pcs each
2 medium sized onions, cut into 4 pcs each
1 tsp cumin
1 onion, finely chopped
1 tbsp ginger-garlic paste
Little oil for cooking
¼ cup fresh tomato puree
1 tomato, chopped finely
1tsp chilli powder, 1 tsp kasoori methi
1 tsp Kitchen King masala or curry powder
2 tbsp fresh cream
A pinch of yellow colour

2 tbsp cashewnuts – 1 tsp dried melon seeds (grind 10 pieces of cashewnuts and 1 tsp of dried melon seeds with a little bit of water to make a dropping consistency paste)
A handful of fresh coriander
Salt and pepper to taste
Garam masala for garnishing

Method

1. Heat 1 tablespoon oil in a heavy-duty pan, add the cumin, finely chopped onion, ginger-garlic paste and stir fry over high flame for 5 minutes.
2. Then add the tomato puree, chopped tomato and sliced onions to the mixture and cook for another 5 minutes or till the gravy leaves oil from the sides. Now add the cashewnut-melon paste.
3. After 5 minutes add the other spices, 1 cup water to make the gravy and then the mushrooms. Cook for 5 minutes. Finally add the cream and fresh coriander.
4. Sprinkle the *garam masala* and serve with hot *paranthas*.

Indian

Subz Biryani

Serves 8

Ingredients

*4 cups cooked rice
2 cups boiled and assorted vegetables
(cauliflower, carrot, French beans and potato)
3 onions, finely sliced
2 tomatoes, finely chopped
2 tbsp ginger-garlic paste
1 tsp Kitchen King masala or curry powder
¼ tsp garam masala
½ tsp chilli powder
Little oil for cooking*

Kharra masala (2 bay leaves, 4 peppercorns, 4 cloves)
¼ tsp each of cardamom powder and cinnamon powder
½ cup paneer cubes
A few blobs of butter
½ cup of milk mixed with a few strands of saffron
Salt and pepper to taste

Method

1. Take 1 tablespoon oil in a pan, add the *kharra masala* and the ginger-garlic paste and onions. Stir fry for 2 minutes, till slightly golden.
2. Add the tomatoes and all the other dry spices and cook till the oil separates.
3. Now add the boiled vegetables and paneer cubes, cook for 7-8 minutes. Take off the fire and keep aside.

How to arrange the biryani

Take an ovenproof dish and grease the bottom. Put a layer of vegetable mixture and then a layer of plain rice over it. Add a few blobs of butter at random over the rice and then sprinkle a little bit of saffron milk on it. Follow the same steps again by arranging the vegetable mix, rice, butter and saffron milk in this very order. Keep layering till all is consumed. The top layer should be of the plain rice with just a spoon of vegetable mix in the centre to give colour. Cover it with a silver foil and bake at 180°C for 20 minutes. Serve hot with plain curd or *raita*.

Aaloo Bahaar

Serves 6

Ingredients

10 potatoes, cut into halves
1 tbsp ginger-garlic paste
5 onions, cut into rings
A handful of coriander, finely chopped
1 tsp red chilli powder
1 tsp garam masala
Juice of 1 lemon
½ tsp coriander powder
Oil for deep frying the potatoes
2 tbsp ghee for cooking the dish
Salt to taste

Method

1. Heat the oil in a heavy-duty pan and deep fry the potatoes till golden brown. Drain and keep aside.
2. In a separate pan heat 2 tablespoons of ghee. Saute the ginger-garlic paste in it, till it leaves a raw smell.
3. Then add the onion rings and cook for 5 minutes, till they become translucent.
4. Add all the masalas and toss in the fried potatoes.
5. Add the coriander and lemon juice. Toss well. Take off the fire and serve hot.

← *Aaloo Bahaar (p 59)*

Indian

Khus Mehak

Makes 4-6

Ingredients

100 ml concentrated khus syrup
A handful of chopped mint leaves
15 ice-cubes
1 tbsp roasted cumin powder
Juice of 2 lemons
2 tbsp castor sugar
2 bottles chilled soda water
Chat masala to taste
A few mint leaves for garnishing

Method

1. Blend all the ingredients in a mixie, except the soda water, for 3-4 minutes.
2. Transfer into a bowl and add the soda water.
3. Pour it into tall glasses and garnish with the mint leaves.
4. Serve chilled.

Firnee

Serves 6

Ingredients

4½ cups milk
3 drops rose essence
A pinch of saffron (5-6 strands)
6 tbsp sugar
5 tbsp rice soaked in water for half an hour
½ tsp cardamom powder
A few chopped almonds for garnishing

Method

1. Put the milk in a heavy-duty pan and heat for 10 minutes.
2. Soak the rice in about ¼ cup water for half an hour. Then blend the rice with the water in a mixie to make the rice milk, and strain. Repeat this process of straining 2-3 times.
3. Now slowly add the rice milk to the milk and cook for 15 minutes on low flame. Stir continuously.
4. Then add the sugar, cardamom powder and saffron. Cook for 2 minutes, till the sugar dissolves. Remove from the heat and cool for 30 minutes and then add the essence.
5. The mixture becomes thick like custard. If there are any lumps on cooling just blend it in a mixie to make it smooth. Now put it in any kind of serving bowls and garnish with the chopped almonds. Refrigerate. Serve chilled.

ITALIAN

> **"Cuisine is only about making foods taste the way they are supposed to taste."**
> – Charlie Trotter Aah

Italy has a great variety of foods, an endless selection of delectable dishes to choose from. Pasta is very popular, and it is a healthy, natural food that offers great scope for quick, tasty and economical meals. Equally well known are pizzas, with a multitude of different toppings. But Italian cooking is much more than just pastas and pizzas.

Here are some mouth-watering recipes.

Menu

- Crispy Fritters (Starter)
- Potato Salad (Salad)
- Spaghetti with Concasse Sauce (Main course)
- Hot Shoppe Pizza (Main course)
- Live Station Pasta (Main course)
- Hot Chocolate Fudge Pudding (Dessert)

Crispy Fritters

Makes about 20

Ingredients

2 large potatoes, peeled and grated
1 can corn kernels (250 gms), drained
½ cup dried breadcrumbs
1 cup spring onions, chopped
1 tsp garam masala
Oil for deep frying

For the dipping sauce

2/3 cup plain yoghurt
2 tbsp fresh chopped mint
2 tsp sweet chilli sauce

Method

1. Mix the ingredients for the dipping sauce and keep aside.
2. Drain the grated potatoes on a paper towel and sqeeze out the excess moisture.
3. Combine the potatoes with all the other ingredients, except the oil.
4. Heat some oil in a heavy-duty pan and spoon out this mixture in small portions into it. Cook over medium heat for 2 minutes on each side or until golden brown.
5. Drain and serve it with the dipping sauce.

Italian

Potato Salad

Serves 8

Ingredients

4 potatoes boiled, peeled and cut into cubes
2 onions, finely chopped
1 capsicum, finely chopped
Generous amount of butter
1 tbsp garlic paste
Salt and white pepper to taste
Parsley for garnishing

For the dressing

1/2 cup each of eggless mayonnaise and hung curd
1/4 tsp mustard powder and 1 tbsp vinegar

← *Spaghetti with Concasse Sauce (p 73)*

Method

1. Heat the butter in a pan. Add the garlic paste. Then add the onions and cook till translucent. Then add the potatoes and capsicum.
2. Toss over high flame for 5 minutes. Season with salt and pepper and take off the fire.
3. Mix the ingredients for the dressing and add to the potato mix.
4. Sprinkle some parsley and serve.

Spaghetti with Concasse Sauce

Serves 8

Ingredients

1 packet spaghetti
1 tsp of oil
A dash of salt

Method

1. Boil a large pan of water with ¾ teaspoon of oil and a dash of salt.
2. Add the spaghetti to it. Let it boil till it becomes soft, approximately for 10 minutes. Then run cold water through it.
3. Apply the remaining ¼ teaspoon oil to the spaghetti so that it does not become sticky.

For the sauce

6 tomatoes, blanched and pureed
½ cup onions, chopped
250 ml tomato puree (preferably readymade)
1 packet soya nutri keema
2 tsp garlic paste, 2 tsp oregano
100 ml olive oil
1 tsp red chilli powder
2 tsp Italian curry powder (can be substituted with
Indian curry powder, for e.g., Kitchen King)
Cornflour paste (1 tsp cornflour mixed with 1 tbsp water)
500 ml of vegetable stock or plain water
3 tbsp finely chopped fresh coriander
A few blobs of butter
Salt and pepper to taste
Parmesan cheese powder for garnishing

Method

1. Soak the soya nutree *keema* in warm water for an hour. Squeeze out the excess water and keep the nutree aside.
2. In a wok, pour the oil, add the chopped onions and garlic paste. Saute for 7-8 minutes
3. Add the soaked soya to it and cook for 10-12 minutes or till it turns red. If the nutri keema sticks to the wok, add some more oil.
4. Add salt and pepper and also the red chilli powder.
5. Add the blanched and pureed tomatoes and cook for another 7 minutes. Stir occasionally.
6. Then add the tomato puree and curry powder.
7. Cook for 2 minutes. Then add the water or vegetable stock and let it simmer on medium heat for 10 minutes.
8. Add the cornflour mix to the gravy and keep stirring for a minute. Finally add the herbs.

9. Garnish the sauce with the fresh coriander.
10. Put the butter cubes on top of the sauce while serving it with the spaghetti.
11. Sprinkle some Parmesan cheese powder on top for a richer taste. (Optional)
12. Serve hot.

Note:
- *It is best to have it with garlic bread.*

Italian

Hot Shoppe Pizza

Serves 4

Ingredients

1 readymade pizza base
2 onions, finely chopped
2 tbsp olive oil
½ cup soft corn kernels
½ cup finely chopped mushrooms
1 yellow bell pepper and red bell pepper, each finely chopped
3 tbsp black olives, 1 tbsp dried oregano
¾ cup tomato puree
½ tsp chilli flakes
½ tsp each of freshly ground garlic and chilli paste
¼ cup mozzarella cheese, grated
Salt and pepper to taste

Method

1. Heat the oil in a pan, add the garlic paste, chilli paste and onions. Saute for 5 minutes.
2. Add the mushrooms, corn, salt, pepper, chilli flakes and oregano and cook further for 5 minutes.
3. Add the tomato puree and bring to the boil or till it thickens.
4. Now take the pizza base and spread this mix over the base. Make sure that the mix is dry.
5. Top this with the black olives and spread the cheese evenly over this topping.
6. Bake at 180°C for 20 - 25 minutes, or till the base is crisp.
7. Cut into slices and serve.

Hot Shoppe Pizza (p 77) →

Italian

Live Station Pasta

Serves 6

Ingredients

3 cups boiled penne pasta
3 capsicums, cut lengthwise
2 tomatoes, deseeded and cut lengthwise
¾ cup mushrooms, boiled and cut lengthwise
1 cup spinach sauce
1 cup Italino sauce
¾ cup fresh cream
Bread croutons for garnishing

For the spinach sauce

1 tbsp butter
1 tbsp flour
1 ½ cups milk
A pinch of mustard powder
½ cup boiled and pureed spinach
Salt and pepper to taste

Method

1. Take a pan. Heat the butter. Add the flour and cook for a minute.
2. Then gradually add the milk, stirring continuously so that it does not form lumps.
3. Then season this mix. Add the pureed spinach to it.
4. Bring to the boil and keep aside.

For Italino sauce

5 tomatoes, blanched and pureed
½ cup chopped onions
1 tsp oregano
1 tsp crushed garlic
2 tsp red wine (optional)
2 tbsp olive oil
Salt and pepper to taste

Method

1. Pour the olive oil into a pan, add the onions and garlic and saute for 2 minutes.
2. Add the pureed tomatoes and, let it simmer on medium heat for 5 minutes. Stir occasionally.
3. Add all the other ingredients and bring to the boil. Keep aside.

Method for assembling the pasta

1. Take 2-3 tablespoons butter in a pan and saute the mushrooms. Add the capsicum, tomatoes, oregano and salt and pepper. Add the pasta. Cook for 5 minutes.
2. Add both the sauces mentioned above, one by one, and toss well. Then add the cream.
3. Remove from the fire and transfer to a bowl. Garnish it with the fried bread croutons.

Note:
- *Make sure to take a non-stick pan for assembling the pasta.*

Italian

Hot Chocolate Fudge Pudding

Serves 6

Ingredients

1 cup flour
2 tsp baking powder
¼ tsp salt
¾ cup sugar
6 tbsp cocoa powder
2 tbsp melted butter
½ cup walnuts
1 cup brown sugar
1+ ¾ cup hot water
½ cup hot milk

Method

1. Sift the dry ingredients, except for the brown sugar, in a deep dish bowl.
2. Add the butter and milk and mix the walnuts.
3. Now sprinkle the brown sugar on top and pour very hot water, from a distance, into the bowl, along the sides and on top. Do not mix. Let the water seep in. Make sure the water is poured from all angles of the dish.
4. Bake at 180°C for 40-45 minutes.
5. Serve hot with vanilla ice-cream.

MEXICAN

**"Any country you want to get into the heart of,
you really have to do it through food."**

– Lula Bertran

Variations in Mexican cuisine allow you to select the type and amount of seasonings most suited to your taste. Certain foods are basic to Mexican cuisine, such as corn, beans, rice, flour, chilli peppers and cheese. These items are combined with each other, or other foods and seasonings to make a wonderful variety of dishes.

Menu

- Chunky Salsa Dip (Sauce)
- Deluxe Nachos (Starter)
- Mushroom 'n' Spinach Empanaditas (Main course)
- Rice Mexicali (Main course)
- Vegetable Burritos (Main course)
- Fried Ice-cream (Dessert)

Mexican

Chunky Salsa Dip

Makes 3½ cups

Ingredients

---

2 tbsp olive oil
1 cup coarsely chopped onions
1 cup coarsely diced capsicum
1 cup coarsely chopped tomatoes
1 tbsp lemon juice
2 tsp Tabasco sauce
½ tsp salt
2 tbsp chopped coriander
½ cup tomato juice

Method

1. Heat the oil in a large pan over high heat. Add the onions and capsicums and saute for 5-6 minutes, stirring frequently until tender.
2. Add the tomatoes and tomato juice. Bring to the boil over high heat. Reduce the heat and simmer for 8 minutes, stirring occasionally until the mixture is slightly thickened.
3. Remove from the heat, stir in the lime juice, Tabasco sauce and salt.
4. Cool to lukewarm and stir in the coriander. Spoon the salsa into a clean jar.
5. Serve with nachos or raw salad.

Note:
- *Salsa can be preserved in a refrigerator for 5-6 days.*

Mexican

Deluxe Nachos

Serves 6

Ingredients

2½ cups soft corn kernels
3 tbsp mixed spices and seasoning (oregano, thyme, chilli powder, pepper any other available herb, mixed proportionately)
¼ cup salsa
¼ cup sliced and drained green olives
1 large tomato, chopped
1 cup shredded processed cheese
1 pkt chips (nachos), easily available in the market
Some spring onions for garnishing

← *Mushroom 'n' Spinach Empanaditas (p 94)*

For the sour cream

100 gms fresh cream

1 tbsp thick curd

A pinch of salt

¼ tsp lemon juice

A little bit of chopped coriander (optional)

First beat the cream and then add all the other ingredients.

Method

1. In a medium pan, take some oil and saute the corn with the spices. Mix well. Cook for 5 minutes and take off the fire.

2. In a large shallow ovenproof dish arrange the chips, topped with the corn mix and cheese.

3. Bake in the oven for 10 minutes or till the cheese melts.
4. Now top it with the olives and salsa. Sprinkle some spring onions on top.
5. Serve with the sour cream.

Mushroom 'n' Spinach Empanaditas

Serves 10

Ingredients

*2 tbsp vegetable oil
1 onion, finely chopped
1 tsp minced garlic
¼ tsp ground cinnamon
½ tsp pepper
200 gms each of mushrooms and spinach, boiled and finely chopped
3 tbsp chopped stuffed olives
½ cup chopped tomatoes
½ tsp chilli powder
Cold milk for glazing
Salt to taste*

Method

1. Heat 2 tablespoons oil in a pan, add the onion and cook for 5 minutes or till tender. Stir in the garlic, cinnamon, chilli powder and pepper. Cook for 30 seconds.
2. Add the mushrooms, stirring frequently for 5 minutes or till the mushrooms begin to brown. Then add the spinach and cook for 8-10 minutes.
3. Stir in the olives and tomatoes, increase the flame to high and cook for 2-3 minutes or till the mixture is reasonably dry. Keep aside.

For the dough

2 cups flour
1 tsp baking powder
1 tsp salt
¾ cup butter, cut into cubes
4 tbsp ice-cold water

Method

1. In a large bowl, combine the dry ingredients. Add the butter and work the mixture till it resembles coarse crumbs.
2. Then add the water, 1 tablespoon at a time, until the dough begins to hold together. Transfer to a lightly floured surface and knead lightly to form a ball. Refrigerate for 10 minutes. Keep aside.

How to assemble the empanaditas

1. Sprinkle some flour on the surface, roll out the pastry dough with a rolling pin on the dusted surface. Cut, as many possible 6" squares with a biscuit cutter or a knife.
2. Place 1-2 teaspoons filling in the centre of each square and fold all the four sides to reach the centre to enclose the filling. Crimp the edges together to seal well.

3. Take a baking tray and grease the bottom of the tray with the butter.
4. Carefully transfer the empanaditas with a metal spatula on the tray.
5. Glaze the cold milk on both the sides of the empanaditas with a brush. Bake for 12-15 minutes until golden.
6. Serve warm.

Mexican

Rice Mexicali

Serves 8

Ingredients

2 cups rice
4 cups water
1 cup thick onion rings
1 cup thick capsicum rings
1 cup sliced tomatoes
¼ cup French beans, finely chopped
1 cup chopped cabbage
1 tsp garlic paste
2 tsp soya sauce
4 tsp chilli sauce
1 tbsp lemon juice

Rice Mexicali →

½ cup oil
2 tbsp white vinegar
½ cup chopped spring onion leaves
¼ cup processed cheese
Salt and pepper to taste

Method

1. Heat some oil. Cook the onions till golden brown. Transfer to a bowl.
2. Now add the capsicum and cook for 2 minutes. Take it out from the pan and keep aside.
3. In the same oil, add the garlic paste and saute for 1-2 minutes. Now add the rice and salt and pepper. Cook till done.
4. Take a separate pan and heat 2 tablespoons oil. Add the spring onion leaves and saute for 3 minutes on high flame.

5. Then add the tomatoes, cooked onions, cooked capsicum and all the sauces. Cook for 5 minutes. Take off the heat, add the lemon juice and cabbage.
6. Add this prepared mixture to the cooked rice. Mix well. Top it with a generous amount of cooking cheese and bake for 10 minutes, till the cheese melts.
7. Sprinkle the finely chopped French beans.
8. Serve hot with tortillas, salsa or sour cream.

Vegetable Burritos

Makes about 12

Ingredients

2 tbsp olive oil
2 medium onions, thinly sliced
1 tbsp chilli powder
1 tsp minced garlic
2 tsp oregano, 1 tsp ground cumin
¾ cup boiled kidney beans
1 cup corn kernels, 6 flour tortillas
1 capsicum, finely chopped
½ cup boiled and chopped potatoes
2 tbsp lime juice
¾ cup processed cheese
Sour cream and salsa for serving

For the flour tortillas

400 gms flour
200 gms wheat flour
2 tbsp cornflour
½ tbsp baking powder
4 tsp oil
½ tsp salt
Lukewarm water

Method

1. Combine all the ingredients and make a dough, adding a little lukewarm water at a time, till it forms a soft dough (firm enough to roll out).
2. Divide the dough into 12 balls and roll into thin circles. Heat a frying pan and cook these tortillas by roasting on both sides. Keep aside.

Method

1. Heat some oil in a pan over medium heat. Cook the onions for 10 minutes, stirring often until golden.
2. Add the chilli powder, garlic, cumin and oregano and stir for a minute. Add 1 tablespoon water, stir and remove from the heat.
3. Add the potatoes, beans, corn, capsicum and lime juice.
4. Spoon 2 tablespoons cheese in the centre of each tortilla, top it with the filling. Fold all the four sides around the filling to enclose.
5. Place the burritos seam side down. Seal the edges with the flour paste and deep fry them in hot oil till crisp. Drain and serve hot with the salsa and sour cream.

Fried Ice-Cream

Serves 8

Ingredients

8-9 firm scoops of vanilla ice-cream
½ cup desiccated shredded coconut
½ cup fine breadcrumbs
1 cup thin consistency sugar syrup
Oil for deep frying

For coating the batter

2 tbsp cornflour
2-3 tbsp flour
A pinch of salt
1 tsp oil
Water to make a thick paste

Method

1. For making the batter mix all the ingredients together, except for the water. Then add the water little by little, to make a thick paste. Keep aside.
2. Mix the desiccated coconut and breadcrumbs in a bowl.
3. Take very firm scoops of vanilla ice-cream and dip them, one by one, in the prepared batter.
4. Roll each ice-cream ball in the breadcrumb mixture.
5. Arrange these on a steel plate and freeze for half an hour till completely firm.
6. Take it out from the freezer and again dip each ice-cream ball in the batter, followed by a coating of the breadcrumb mixture. Now freeze again for at least 1 hour.

7. Pour the oil in a wok and heat till it smokes. Add 2 ice-cream balls at a time and fry them for less than a minute or till the outer covering becomes brown. Repeat the process with the remaining ice-cream scoops.

8. After frying the ice-cream balls, dip them for a fraction of second in the sugar syrup and immediately take them out. Serve immediately.

Note:
- *Make sure that the ice-cream is very firm and hard or it will melt during the cooking process.*

THAI

> **"The preparation of good food is merely another expression of art, one of the joys of civilized living."**
> – Dione Lucas

With the growing availability of Thai ingredients, Thai cuisine has become popular with most people. Thai food strikes a balance between sweet, sour, hot, bitter and salty. The widely used ingredients in Thai cooking are - hot chillies, garlic, lemon grass, fish sauce and coconut. The word Thai means 'free' and Thai cooks always add their own special touches to every dish. A typical Thai meal consists of a soup, salad, a stir fry, any kind of curry, rice and a dessert. Thai cuisine is considered one of the more nutritious cuisines, as most of the dishes are quickly cooked so as to preserve the nutrients.

Menu

- Thai Cheese Cake (Starter)
- Tom Yum Soup (Soup)
- Thai Red Curry (Main course curry dish)
- Phad Phak (Stir fry)
- Coconut Custard (Dessert)

Thai Cheese Cake

Serves 6

Ingredients

6 bread slices
1 cup fresh breadcrumbs
1 tsp each of finely chopped green and red chillies
1 tsp finely chopped garlic
1 tsp ginger, thinly sliced
1 cup thick cream
2 tsp chopped coriander leaves
½ cup paneer
Oil for shallow frying
Salt and pepper to taste

Method

1. Mix all the ingredients, except the oil, in a bowl.
2. Divide the mixture into small portions and roll into flat round cakes.
3. Heat the oil in a pan and shallow fry the cakes on medium heat till crisp and golden on both sides.
4. Serve hot on a bed of lettuce leaves with chilli sauce.

Tom Yum
(Spicy Thai vegetable soup)

Serves 4

Ingredients

700 ml vegetable stock
1 tbsp lemon grass in the dried and concentrated form
50 gms basil leaves
20 gms chopped green chillies
100 gms boiled and chopped fresh mushrooms
2 spring onions, finely chopped
100 ml fresh lime juice
30 gms red curry paste
Salt to taste
A few coriander leaves for garnishing

Method

1. Add the lemon grass, basil leaves and green chillies to the vegetable stock and bring to the boil.
2. Add the red curry paste, salt, mushrooms and spring onions and simmer for 10 minutes.
3. Add the lemon juice and serve piping hot, garnished with the coriander leaves.

Note:
- *To make 700 ml of vegetable stock, use 4 vegetable stock cubes mixed with 700 ml of water. Crumble the cubes in water over medium flame, and simmer till dissolved.*

Thai Red Curry

Serves 6

Ingredients

2 cups assorted vegetables (mushrooms, French beans, carrots, cauliflower)
4 tbsp readymade red curry vegetable paste
2 tbsp vinegar, 3 tbsp oil
2 tbsp vegetable fish sauce
A few basil leaves
2 tbsp dried or fresh chopped lemon grass
7-8 kaffir lime leaves, (in dried and concentrated form)
1 glass vegetable stock
2 glasses of coconut milk
Salt to taste

Method

1. Take some oil in a wok, add the chopped lemon grass. Stir fry the red curry paste for 5 minutes on medium flame. Make sure that the paste does not stick to the bottom.
2. Then add all the vegetables. Stir fry for 5 minutes, adding ¼ cup of coconut milk.
3. Add the lemon grass, basil and lime leaves and salt, let it cook for 5 minutes.
4. Add in the remaining coconut milk, stock and boil for 10 minutes.
5. Then add the vinegar and fish sauce and boil for 5 minutes.
6. Serve hot with plain boiled rice.

Note:
- *To make the coconut milk, grate one coconut, removing the brown covering and churn it in a mixie, using enough water to make it milky. Strain through a muslin cloth. Throw away the waste coconut and keep aside the coconut milk. One can also use readymade coconut milk available in the market.*

Phad Phak
(Stir fried vegetables Thai style)

Serves 4

Ingredients

3 tbsp oil
2 tsp finely chopped garlic
100 gms baby corn
½ cup boiled and chopped mushrooms
¼ cup French beans, chopped lengthwise
1" pcs galangal, 2 tsp red curry paste
100 ml vegetable stock
1 tbsp dark soya sauce
1 tbsp vegetable fish sauce
½ cup red capsicum, chopped lengthwise
Salt and pepper to taste

Method

1. Heat 3 tablespoons oil in a wok. Add the garlic and red curry paste. Then add the galangal and saute for 3-4 minutes.
2. Add all the vegetables and stir fry for 5-7 minutes.
3. Add the soya sauce, vegetable stock, fish sauce and salt and pepper and cook for 5 minutes, till all the stock dries up.

Note:
- *To make it more spicy, increase the proportion of red curry paste.*

Coconut Custard

Serves 8

Ingredients

500 ml coconut milk
½ cup castor sugar
¼ tsp nutmeg powder
¼ tsp cinnamon powder
Cornflour paste (2 tsp cornflour mixed with 2 tbsp water)
A few drops of vanilla essence
¼ cup dessicated coconut powder
½ cup fresh cream
½ cup coconut cream

Method

1. Heat the coconut milk and add the sugar. Cook on medium heat till the sugar dissolves.
2. Add the nutmeg, cinnamon and vanilla essence and bring to the boil. Then add in the coconut cream and cornflour paste. Cook on low heat till the paste thickly coats the back of the spoon. Cool. Stir in the fresh cream. Spoon this mix into the glasses. Let it chill thoroughly.
3. Sprinkle the dessicated coconut on it. Serve this with fresh fruits.